But I Don't Want to Be the President

Were the American People Listening?

REV. DR. McNAIR RAMSEY

DORRANCE
PUBLISHING CO
EST. 1920
PITTSBURGH, PENNSYLVANIA 15238

Dorrance Publishing Co
585 Alpha Drive
Pittsburgh, PA 15238
Visit our website at *www.dorrancebookstore.com*

ISBN: 978-1-6376-4094-4
ESIBN: 978-1-6376-4936-7

BOOK DEDICATION

I have been honored and blessed to be permitted as an educator and administrator to play an influential role in the lives of so many students from elementary to college age. Serving in such roles has brought me much joy and one of these joys is to see the students descend and walk across the stages and receive their degrees. This never ceases to bring a smile to my face and great joy to my heart.

Because of the achievement of the students, I dedicate this book to all the students that I may have influenced and played a small role in assisting them in reaching their educational goals and taking their places in society to help others. I pray that they continue to bring joy to others as they have brought joy to me.

ACKNOWLEDGEMENT

Isaac Newton stated: "If I have seen farther, it is by standing on the shoulders of giants." I have stood and I am standing on the shoulders of giants. Those giants are Mrs. Phyllis Richardson who retired from the former Concordia College Alabama, located in Selma, Alabama and served as Academic Dean and did most of the proofreading of this writing. I am standing on the shoulders of my oldest daughter, Dr. Jennifer Ramsey who is a teacher in Lee County Elementary School located in Auburn, Alabama. She gave valuable encouragement to pursue the writing of the book and I appreciated her wisdom. A special thanks to my granddaughter, JoNaira Wilkins who is a recent graduate from Sanford University located in Birmingham, Alabama, and who stated: "The book had great potentials and should be completed." Finally to a good friend Mrs. Gwendolyn Moore, Associate Director of Admissions and Recruitment at Alabama State University, Montgomery, Alabama who always said to me: "Dr. You should place your thoughts in a book."

Thank you, family and friends, for your valuable words of encouragement, assistants, dedicated work and just being there in a time of need. You mean so much to me and to the completion of this writing.

INTRODUCTION

There is a Spiritual Song composed by Kurt Carr and the lyrics by Lilly Mack Music Kcartunes: The title of the song is: "I Almost Let Go." Though only the first eleven lines speak to where my emotions, feelings and concerns were with regards to the elected 45th President of the United States, and the lack of any leadership for the last four years, the song addresses my feelings and so, I will share all of the words of the song to give earned justice to the same as it speaks so well to life and may be of help to those who read this book.

The Song
"I almost let go
I felt like I couldn't take life anymore
My problems had me bound
Depression weighed me down
But God held me close
So I wouldn't let go
God's mercy kept me
So I wouldn't let go

I almost gave up
I was right at the edge of a breakthrough
But I couldn't see it

The devil really had me
But Jesus came and grabbed me
And he held me close so I wouldn't let go
God's mercy kept me so I wouldn't let go
So I am here today because God kept me
I'm alive today, only because of His grace

Oh, he kept me, God kept me, He kept me
So I wouldn't let go

I almost let go
I felt like I couldn't take life anymore
My problems had me bound
Depression weighed me down

But God held me close
So I wouldn't let go
God's mercy kept me
So I wouldn't let go

So I'm here today because God kept me
I'm alive today only because of His grace
Oh, He kept me, God kept me
God kept me, He kept me
So I wouldn't let go
He kept me, God kept me, He kept me
God kept me, He kept me
So I wouldn't let go"

As stated earlier, the song's first eleven lines speak to my need to put in writing my feelings relating to the need to write this book. Out of a very deep concern, and disappointments relating to the election and subsequent lack of positive leadership of our 45th President and how very gifted, intelligent, smart, and well thinking Americans could elect such a person to the highest and most influential position in the world is mind boggling. Also, I wanted to make use of the time given to me and my family due to the coronavirus "stay at home mandate" to help keep the virus from spreading.

My deep concerns for the democracy of America, though not always adhering to those things written in the constitution, at least ever-so-often the leadership would make an attempt to get back on track. Donald Trump did not.

My deep concern for an America that for the most part had a visceral decency about it and wanted to do what is decent in helping others. Donald Trump didn't meet the call.

My belief that we had an America that had always fought for the well-being of others in this country and the countries of the world. Yet here we were trying to build walls to keep people from coming into America. Again, our President failed to help anyone but himself.

Our 45th President not denouncing hate groups but encouraging them and causing them to come out of their hiding after being asleep for thirteen to seventeen years as the Cicadas do at a period of time. The 45th President made use of his time awaking those who would bring an embarrassment to themselves, himself, and to our country.

All this was being threatened and left me with the feeling of wanting to give up. Thus the book:

BUT I DON'T WANT TO BE THE PRESIDENT

Were the American People Listening?

There are very few parents, if any at all, that are parents who have not heard the words: "But I don't want to!" Most parents and especially those who have dealt with toddlers can be a witness to these words: "But I don't want to."

My wife, a retired preschool teacher for over twenty-plus years, and I raised three beautiful daughters, and we are the proud grandparents of five. We have heard such words many times.

These words are spoken with no regards to what is being asked by the parent. However, with all due respect to the toddlers, they do not ascribe, in most cases, to what is best for them. They simply want to prolong the time to engage in the activity in which they are invested.

Note, if you would, how such a statement is assigned to these precious little ones?

Parent(s): "It is time to come in from your outside playing."

Toddler: "But I don't want to."

Parent: "It is time to take your bath and or get cleaned up."

Toddler: "But I don't want to."

Parent: "It is time to put your play toys away."

Toddler: "But I don't want to."

Parent: "It is time to eat your meal."

Toddler: "But I don't want to."

Parent: "It is time to rest or it's time to go to bed."

Toddler: "But I don't want to."

Parent: "It is time for us to go."

Toddler: "But I don't want to."

On and on the scenario goes and if it were left up to the toddler, the engagement would never end. These scenarios are a good indication of the importance of parents guiding their toddlers toward what is best for the toddlers. Yet, toddlers, even at a young age, feel they know what's best for them. President Trump is not a child; however, he, by his actions or lack of action, communicates to those he serves that he does not want to be the president. He has not asked himself that important question former President John F. Kennedy asked the American people in one of his speeches: "Ask not what your country can do for you, ask what you can do for your country." This President has used the American people and the position of the office to advance his own personal wellbeing and not that of the people and the nation. He has instead asked: "What can my country do for me?"

It then behooves us to observe some of his actions which can be converted into the words of: "BUT I DON'T WANT TO BE THE PRESIDENT."

During a segment of his 2015 campaign, the President spoke what he thought he was stating secretly before departing the campaign bus.

"They will let you do anything to them. You can run your hand up their dress or grab them........." This kind of remark only supports the commitment that to vote for and elect as well as attempt to reelect a person of this caliber sends the signal that it is ok to violate my wife, daughter, sister, and my neighbor's female relatives.

What does this say to the right-minded voters of America? "But I don't want to.."

When he shared with the American people that he would walk into the dressing room(s) of contestants unannounced and some of the young women would not be dressed or half dressed, this demonstrates that he had no respect for the privacy of women. What was he saying to the right-minded American people? "But I don't want to..............."

When several females came forward and shared their sexual encounters with the President, and it is common knowledge that he paid hush money to at least one and perhaps more (we do not know for sure, as we have not been able to see his financial report as of yet), what are his actions/or lack thereof telling right-minded voters? "But I don't want to................................"

When the leader of the greatest democratic country in the world can lie thousands of times standing before the American people, what is he saying to the right-minded voters of this country? "But I don't want to................."

When a chosen leader chooses to degrade those who have personal and/or physical challenges, i.e., speech impediment, body control, mental handicaps or some other challenges they must cope with, and the President mocks them before a national audience, what does the President communicate to the right-minded audience? "But I don't want to.."

When the leader of this great American nation sides with the White Supremacy group and refuses to denounce David Duke but instead takes the side of the KKK in Charlottesville, Va. who attacked demonstrators, calling them good people, demonstrates that he is on the side of a terrorist organization. Just what is the President communicating to the right-minded voters? "But I don't want to…………….."

When the leader of the free world practices the tactics of the German Nazi and the tactics of Fascist in separating immigrants and children from their parents and placing them in cages or behind prison walls, it requires the question: What is this saying to the right-minded American people? "But I don't want to……………"

When the Commanding Chief speaks derogatory remarks toward Generals and other Gold Star Officers and highly decorated service men and women, who place their lives on the line so that Americans and other nations can remain free, what is this saying to the right-minded American voters? "But I don't want to…………………"

It doesn't take much to have a leader to practice the ways of the Nazi/Fascist/Communist Leaders. It is an easy thing to ascribe to when you have no conscience or if you have one, it is an excusing one or it is a dead conscience, which allows one to ascribe to such. It allows one to treat people in the most horrible manner and not care about them having a job, a place to live, health insurance, equal wages, equal rights, the right to vote and the right to protest peacefully. Such a nonfunctioning conscious person, a so-called leader, can only blame others. He excuses himself by saying that everything said about him is fake news or claims he doesn't know anything about the situation or according to him it is a hoax. When a leader reflects that he is absentminded and cannot remember that he did such things, what is he communicating to the right-minded voters of the nation? "But I don't want to…………… ……………………"

When a chosen leader chooses not to give attention to the previously elected leaders' exit recommendations/interviews and more or less throws the plan book away and has nothing prepared to take its place for attacking things that can devastate our nation such as expected vi-

ruses/diseases and or attacks, and he trashes the play book mostly because he has a dislike for those leaving office and as a result, look at what our nation is suffering? Yes, the most devastating virus in a hundred years and the leader has no idea as to how to handle the situation, resulting in hundreds of thousands of citizens dying and over fifteen and a half million contracting the virus, what is this saying to the right-minded American people? "But I don't want to.............................
....................."

When all eyes are on the top leadership of the country, the President of the United States, looking to him for directions and leadership, looking to him for examples to follow, and looking to him for sound advice and he has nothing to suggest (not even the modeling of wearing a mask) and all he has to offer is "You are on your own", what does this say to the right-minded people of America?

"But I don't want to..."

One would think that a caring leader would be moved to compassion, and/or moved to showing empathy toward grieving, and hurting people, the twenty million plus that have contracted the disease, the three hundred and fifty thousand who have passed away, the frontline health service people, and those separate from loved ones in the nursing homes and hospitals because of the coronavirus. Yet the leader shows no compassion, no empathy of true feeling and experiencing what his subjects are experiencing. Perhaps one would be correct in saying that President Donald Trump simply does not know what to do and he refuses to allow anyone to give him sound advice on how to address a problem or refuses to accept the sound advice given. When this happens the old adage falls into place: "If you don't care who gets the credit, the job will get done." However, in such a case as this, President Trump would have been credited with the doing of the good advice given to him. Not doing this forces the writer to ask: What does this communicate to right-minded voters in this country?

"But I don't want to..."

When the elected leader of the Republican Party does the opposite of what one of the greatest predecessors of the Republican Party i.e., President Ronald Regan, achieved when he asked Mr. Gorbachev to "tear down that wall" and the wall that separated West and East Germany came down. But President Trump, by any means necessary and at any cost, wants to build walls even if it means taking money from those who were deceived into giving and the money was used to enhance one of his crooked supporters. How can we as a nation tell or encourage other nations to join hands in peace and togetherness when we are building walls? What is this saying to the right-minded voters of the land? "But I don't want to………………….."

When the chosen leader commits to the promise he would choose the best, most gifted persons to work in his cabinet but instead selects crooks, criminals and yes men and women, thus leading the President himself being the chief crook of all. Some of those whom he selected have been found guilty of crimes, or pleaded guilty and sent to prison, or being investigated and/or some leaving because of a poor working relationship with a narcissistic individual, what does this tell right-minded voters about such a leader? "But I don't want to ……………… …………………………."

When the candidate running for the Office of President makes a statement during the campaigning process that he can go out on 5th Avenue and shoot someone and nothing will be done. (He has done everything but shoot someone.) What does this tell right-minded people about the current leader of this country? "But I don't want to…………………."

When a leader employs only such people who are YES individuals and those who agree with everything he says and if you do not "YOU ARE FIRED", what is being communicated to right-minded voters by the leader? "But I don't want to…………………………………….."

When the leader of the United States of America encourages the citizens to take certain medicines i.e., hydroxychloroquine (not following the advice of his medical taskforce) and continues to make unproven, off-the-wall statements about the coronavirus, and chooses not to lead by leadership of wearing a mask, what is this saying to the nation of right-minded voters? "But I don't want to............"

When the sitting President invites foreign nations to engage in the United States elections (China, Russia to name a few) and those responsible for our nation's security discover that the nation of Russia did indeed interfere with our election and the President does not take any action and worse yet does not believe his own nation's intelligence report, what does this say to the right-minded American voters? "But I don't want to......................................"

When the leader of America designs a meeting with a known enemy (Russia) without any other U.S. Representative(s) present, not even an interpreter, and does not convey what was discussed, what does this communicate to the right-minded American people? "But I don't want to..
..............."

When the sitting President engages with another nation and asks a favor for a favor—Quid Pro Quo, something for something—asking that a foreign nation provide dirt or inappropriate conduct on an opponent. What is this saying to the right-minded voters of America? "But I don't want to..."

When the leader of the greatest free country in the world makes no attempt to question, investigate, and/or sanction Russia for placing bounties on the lives of American soldiers and denies that such an act is true: What has he stated in this lack of action on his part? "But I don't want to............"

When the President of the United States orders a group of peaceful demonstrators to be tear gassed so that he can stage a photo op in front of a church at which he held a Bible in an incorrect way—upside down—what does this communicate to the people of America? "But I don't want to..............."

When a leader of a country like the United States who is to set examples for others to follow, especially young boys and girls, instead tells thousands of lies, what does this communicate to the right-minded voters? "But I don't want to be…………………………………………………… ……..."

When the leader of the greatest free country of the world shows disrespect toward the media, even when a news reporter offers him the opportunity to share with the nation by a question of: "What would you say to the American people about the coronavirus?" The President's response was: "I would tell them you are a horrible reporter, what a nasty question." Then he proceeded to say other disrespectful things. What is this communicating to the right-minded voters of this country? "But I don't want to……………………………………………………… ……..."

When the President of the U.S., who has executive powers to order full speed ahead by enacting the Safety Production Act to engage in mass production of PPE for the protection of the American public and front-line medical personnel, does not use this power, what is this communicating to the right-minded people? "But I don't want to…… …………………………………………………… "

In the 244- or 245-year history of this nation, it is not known that any president (even though there were some who were racists and owned slaves) ever played the race card. (Note, President Obama had every reason to play the race card on numerous occasions but did not resort to doing it.) Yet we have President Trump, the leader of our nation who makes every attempt to pit suburbs against the city, the South against the North, and Blacks against the Whites. Matthew 12:25 says to us as a people: "A kingdom/house divided against itself cannot stand" (*KJV*).

When a leader of a free democratic country attempts to divide instead of unite, what does this say to the right-minded people of our nation? "But I don't want to…………"

We are all aware that politics is a dirty business especially when one is vying for a position that others are seeking as well. Those sparring against one another dig up all kinds of dirt on each other, the dirtier the better, the juicier the better, and Donald Trump is good at it. He not only throws everything but the kitchen sink at his opponents, but he also does the same to his friends: i.e., Ted Cruz, Marco Rubio, Mary Trump and Jeff Sessions. We have learned that it is better to be an enemy of Donald Trump than a friend because the saying is indeed true: "With a friend like Donald Trump, who needs an enemy?" When a leader is only concerned about himself and only cares about "ME" and what's in it for me and "MY" businesses, what does this communicate to the right-minded American people? "But I don't want to...............
...................................."

When a selected leader in a position like President of the United States cannot let go of grievance against icons in politics such as the likes of President George W. Bush, Representative John R. Lewis (even when family members do not wish his presence) the least one can do is to speak kind words of comfort to the nation on behalf of the family or send a representative to pay respects. It speaks volumes of negative things about a person when the presence of the one who holds the highest position of the land is not desired at the funeral of a family's loved one. So, when one is so small and cannot bring himself to be kind in the midst of grieving, what does this say to right-minded voters about the leader? "But I don't want to..
........................."

When a leader ignores the truth and refuses to give attention to the Medical Task Force employed by him to give the best advice and that advice is all based on facts which show America is not doing well in getting a handle on the coronavirus pandemic, what does this tell right-minded people about the President? "But I don't want to.........
...."

When a leader knows that he/she is gifted, learned, smart, extraordinary, graduated from a respectable university or college, and has a beautiful family, one does not need to brag about it. Those who know you and those around you will know and show their appreciation. But when you succumb to self-glorification, pointing out how well you scored on a test, and how great your brain is; indeed when you have to toot your own horn, maybe the things you say about yourself or the things you want to persuade others to believe about you, are not true.

When we have a leader who does these things, what does this communicate to the right-minded people about such a person? "But I don't want to…………………………………….."

Theorists and other writers tell us that "Everyone rises to his/her level of incompetence." That is, there is always a task or tasks that one at some point and time cannot perform. The individual, no matter how skilled does not possess the ability to do the job. Donald Trump is not presidential material no matter what he has done in the business world. Even there, his track record is not the greatest as there have been major failures and bankruptcy. When we have a leader who refuses to accept good advice and/or cannot bring himself to say: "I don't know but I will look into it and find out." What does this communicate to right-minded voters? "But I don't want to…………………"

When major allies (we hope they will remain allies) are disappointed and perhaps laughing behind our backs because of the lack of leadership skills of our 45th leader and many fellow countrymen/women just don't want to listen to the President speak, or have him to represent them in public for fear of embarrassment. What does this communicate to the right-minded voters in America?

"But I don't want to……………………………………………"

What has been presented to the reader(s) in this book are but a few of the things done by the President of the United States. If everything he has done was written, one book could not contain all of it. This book for all intent and purpose may be an ongoing text, as President Trump is not finished with his disappointments, doings, and ignorant statements of embarrassments toward the American people. But these will be for another writer to bring to the attention of the people.

However, in addition to all of this, there are several conclusions that we must draw from these actions or versions of what the President has said to the American people: President Donald Trump is not a child, though on many occasions he conducts himself as one. He knows what is only best for HIS personal wellbeing and his businesses but he does not know nor does he care to do what is best for the people of America.

Observe the wrongs committed by this one man? He has:

Wronged our allies all over the world

Wronged the American School Systems

Wronged his cabinet members

Wronged the children of the nation

Wronged the coronavirus families of grieving members

Wronged the coronavirus cases victims

Wronged the frontline workers

Wronged the immigrants

Wronged the institutions of government

Wronged the medical personnel

Wronged the Medical Task Force

Wronged the media

Wronged the military service men and women

Wronged the peaceful demonstrators

Wronged the people of color

Wronged the people of faith

Wronged the physically/mentally challenged

Wronged his political colleagues

Wronged the Republican Party

Wronged all the races of America

Wronged the spirit of the American people

Wronged the senior citizens in care centers

Wronged the states that make up America, i.e., governors

Wronged the voting process

Wronged the USPS (United States Postal Service)

Wronged Women

For the last four years our country has been running itself and existing on past beliefs, events, understandings and know-how. In other words, the United States has been using its reserved gifts and powers because the leadership of President Trump has not done anything to improve or enhance this nation. He has ignored the three branches of the government and has brought this nation down to the lowest level since its beginning. He has ignored the laws of this land and replaced the same with his way of thinking.

Thus, every serious and right-minded citizen must ask him/herself this question: How many wrongs must this one man commit before we say loud and with conviction, "this is enough"?

Perhaps a more pressing question would be: How can any sane (providing Donald Trump is sane) person expect to be reelected as the leader of the American people? Shall we dare say that Donald Trump does not process all of his senses and that he is an insane individual?

I am deeply concerned and in a state of wondering will our America be able to recover from the muck that this president has directed this nation to?

It falls upon every citizen of this nation to seriously study those we are to choose as our leaders: This applies to those of the local, the state, the national, the federal or the world as far as this matter is concerned. We must seriously vet those choosing to serve us and always choose the very best regardless of the political party.

Even though the right to vote is a privilege, it is much more. It is an obligation. Recalling the words of a sainted professor of history of mine and also one of the Courageous Eight—the eight men and women who spearheaded the voters' rights movement in Selma, Alabama—Prof. James Gildersleeve said: "A voteless people is a helpless people." All persons who are of voting age must register to vote and all persons who are registered must vote. Vote every time and do not allow anything but death to hinder one from voting.

Certainly the current President has shown the people that indeed: "Everyone at some point and time comes to his level of incompetence." President Trump has reached his, and he is bringing our country down to the lowest level of any president. Are the American people listening?

It is necessary to remind those of the professional work forces and all who have aspired to a position in life, whether it is through education, or hands-on skills, there were things, certain points of knowing that "this is what I want to do in life". It is an A-HA moment. A moment that we may not have recognized when we were growing up and it didn't come to us until we were doing it for a while. In reflection, we notice with admiration this is why I had to go through this or that. Indeed, I was being made ready for this time in my life.

Sadly, there is no evidence that anything like this occurred in the life of Donald Trump to prepare him for the position that he held. He never served in a local city, state, or national position of leadership. I would doubt that he ever held a college student leadership position, such as SGA, Class President, or civic organization leadership position.

I would submit to the readers that the Fairytale Poem stated below can and should apply to what Donald Trump has done to our nation. I am recalling from memory the poem and hope that I remember it correctly. It goes something like this:

> "Humpty Dumpty sat on a wall
> Humpty Dumpty had a great fall
> All the king's horses and all the king's men
> Couldn't put Humpty Dumpty back together again."

I am not a poet, but I will give it a try in re-phrasing the above poem to reflect what I see President Trump and the leadership of the Republican Party are doing to our country.

> Humpty Trumpty wanted to build a wall
> Humpty Trumpty said, "Mexico would pay for the wall"
> The leadership of the Republican party sat on the wall
> They sat on their fist and reared back on their wrist and didn't make the call to stop the crumbling of America's wall
> And the walls of America tumbled down with a great fall.
> Who will put the wall of America back together again?

Let us not forget that the President has, in a sense, kept his promise of building a wall. He has built and continues to build walls of divisions between people of color and the Caucasian people. He has built walls of division between the migrant children and their parents. He continues to build walls of division between the cities and the suburbs of our nation. He has built walls of division between the law-abiding people of the United States and those pledged to be the protectors of the law. He has built walls of division between the have and the have nots. He has built a wall to encase the U.S. Constitution and keep it from being the document that every American should abide by and replaced it with his Trump constitution.

It becomes necessary to ask: Are the American people listening?

We are truly blessed to be living in the United States of America where the military is friendly toward the government and is not against the citizens of this nation. Though there are a few things that can be questioned such as the use of the military to disperse the crowd in order to stage President Trump's photo op in front of the church. However, it is worth repeating that we are most fortunate not to have a military that stands only on the side of the nation's leadership.

This is important because I am reminded that during the crossing of the Selma, Alabama Edmund Pettus Bridge on the march to Montgomery, the Federal Troops were sent to protect the marchers against the hateful local law enforcement and mean Caucasian citizens. With the disrespect that President Trump has shown toward key military personnel, Generals, Lt. Colonels, Commander of a battleship and those he selected to serve in his cabinet who resigned because they could not see themselves working for someone who does not follow sound advice. Who can the President call friends? This is called to our attention in order to point out that Governor George Wallace about the same time period of the March from Selma to Montgomery stood in the door at the University of Alabama in an attempt to keep African Americans from entering the institution. However, when he was confronted by the Federal Troops and asked to "step aside", he came to attention, saluted, and stepped aside.

President Trump has said that he will not concede the election. He may not, but I would remind the readers that there are troops that can remove him from the White House. He can be taken away in handcuffs and possibly arrested and incarcerated. Are the right-minded American people listening? This man does not wish to be the President.

I would submit to the American people that there is every possibility that President Trump may be a double spy for the Russian government as he gives his support to the enemies on the outside of the nation as well to the same on the inside of the nation. No one would conspire with a foreign leader as Donald Trump does unless he is a double agent or unless Putin is holding something so damming over the head of Trump which makes him not act in the best interest of America unless this was the case.

If there was some way to place an investigative team on the ground of Russia to look into why Russia has such a hold on Trump, I dare to say my intuition suggests to me that such a team would discover that Putin may be blackmailing Trump because he has a love child or children by a Russian woman or women, or perhaps there is a video or some kind of film with Trump engaging in sexual acts with a woman or women from one of his visits to Russia. Indeed, something is being held over the head of Donald Trump to make him so loyal to Putin. It is difficult to believe that someone elected as the leader of this nation, or any right-minded citizen, could come to turn his back on all that America stands for and the allies that have stood by the side of this nation in support of freedom and democracy and become a traitor: Are the right-minded American people listening? This man does not want to be the President.

When President Trump states that what is said about him is all "FAKE NEWS", all fingers are pointed back to him as the guilty party who is the FAKE.

When President Trump says, "All that is being reported or announced about me is a HOAX", it is him that is the HOAXER. When President Trump labels someone to be "A LIAR", he has admitted openly that "it is I who is the LIAR-IN-CHIEF". When President Trump publicly states that a news reporter is a "POOR EXCUSE OF A REPORTER", he lays judgement upon himself that it stands to be understood that he is a POOR EXCUSE OF A LEADER. Whatever words President Trump uses to describe another person, group, or organization are the very words that describe him. Are the right-minded voters of America listening? This man does not desire to be the President and he is a coward for not admitting it openly.

It is certain that President Trump does not desire to be the President of the United States of America and the American people should listen and respond to the words: "BUT I DON'T WANT TO BE THE PRESIDENT OF THE UNITED STATES." These words are true, but what he wants to be is:

Adolph Hitler

Joseph Stalin

Fidel Castro

Benito Mussolini

Kim Jong Un

Vladimir Putin

Or some other dictator, Nazi, authoritarian leader.

Notice if you will, that everything that President Trump wishes or said about someone else had an adverse effect:

This reminds me of the story told in the Bible, the book of Esther. The characters are Queen Esther, Mordecai, Haman, and King Xerxes. The plot by Haman begins in chapter 3 and Haman is hanged on the gallows he built for Mordecai in chapter 7. Certainly this brings to bare the old adage saying: "If you dig a hole for me, you had better dig two. For the one you dig for me may just be meant for you." Thus I ask that you give attention to those things President Trump has tried to place upon another?

He has not been granted a second term, yet he along with other Republicans did their all to try and make sure that President Barack Obama would not receive a second term. He along with permanent Republican leaders plotted on the very night of the inauguration of former President Barack Obama on how they could keep him from serving a second term: Trump failed, they failed. He didn't believe he could contract the coronavirus. He failed and caught it. He wanted to lock up Hillary Clinton and others, now with his Presidency ending, he may very well be locked up. He failed. If we listen to the words a person speaks of himself, his words will tell you something about the person doing the speaking. What he says only reveals what is the truth about who he is and what he stands for: A fake, a liar, a fraud, a rigger, a separatist, and a racist. He shows in character and his actions each and every day that he does not want to be the President of the United States.

Trump has stated through his nonverbal communication that he does not wish to be the President of the United States. Now that the people have granted his nonverbal wish, he does not desire to accept the fact that the people have spoken.

President Donald Trump has reflected that he does not wish to abide by the laws of our land, that is the constitution of the United States. However, this should not be a surprise to anyone because throughout President Trump's four years in office he has not given any serious respect to any of the governing laws.

Still, in spite of his desire to not be the President we had seventy-three million people to think otherwise. They voted for him and this moves me to say the famous words spoken during a space launching: "Houston, we have a problem." Indeed, America, we have a problem.

Such words communicate that something seriously is wrong. To seek to elect someone who has demonstrated that he does not wish to be the President, to elect someone who has shown he is not presidential material, to elect someone whose moral standards are as low as anyone in the nation, to elect someone who is divisive, to elect someone who can't tell the truth, to elect someone who is a manipulator and selfish individual and one who puts people against one another rather than seeking to create unity. Such things send the message sound judgement has been overlooked. It does not make any sense to force a person to do something he does not wish to be or to encourage someone to accept a position that he is incapable of fulfilling. All suggest that America has a problem.

We have a problem because young boys and girls look to the highest office of the nation to model themselves. We have a problem because other nations look to America for guidance and directions. We have a problem because we are the standard bearer to the world.

We have a problem because First Corinthians 15:33 tells us: "Be not deceived: Evil communications corrupt good manners." We have a problem because Abraham Lincoln said in his June 16, 1858 acceptance speech for the Illinois Senate ("House Divided"): "A house divided against itself cannot stand." Our nation at that time was deeply divided over slavery and there was a need for uniting.

Apparently seventy-three million plus voters and 232 electoral votes did not believe. They gave their all to reelect someone whom the experts; those who know about the prospects of winning, such as the pollsters, news reporters, strategists, and mathematicians who stated many times over, that "President Donald Trump cannot win with just his base."

Thus the decision for the Republican Party is: How can it sway eight million plus voters and more electoral votes to come along beside them in order to win the Presidency? Still, seventy-three million plus voters sought to elect someone who by words, actions, lack of skills and standard of life reflected that he did not want to be the President of the United States.

This belief of not wanting to be the President became more evident after the election was over. The man we call President Trump stopped, desisted, quit, ceased, refused to carry out the duties of the Presidency. He instead spent his time golfing, sulking, tweeting, and planning for 2024. Yes, he took a seventy-day vacation while the people suffered. No jobs, no food, sick with the coronavirus, 597,785 at this writing dead from the coronavirus. Indeed, the people have no food: His response would be: "Let them golf." The people have no jobs: "Let them golf," The people are sick. "Let them golf."

So then the question becomes: Will seventy-three million plus standby the impeached, non-reelected, non-conceding manipulator and vote for him in 2024?"

Consider this: No one enjoys being around a brat, only a few people love a brat (perhaps the mother and father of the brat or maybe other brats). Very few people stand by a sore loser, in fact just as well as a person can graciously accept winning, one should also accept losing and plan to fight another day. Thus the way President Trump has and is conducting himself will drive some of his base supporters away and cause a few of his supporters to come to themselves and say: "We will not support this kind of person." Others will come to know what is right and will seek to do it. Yes, there will be those who will stand by him no matter what. They will do this because even though they know better they do not wish to do better.

The situation reveals itself: President Donald Trump will be known as a loser. The question is how many times does he desire to be called a loser? He lost reelection by seven million plus votes, he lost the electoral votes by seventy-four votes, he lost the court lawsuits, and he lost all of the recounts.

Thus it is fitting for me to say, I have always believed and my parents taught their children to believe that there are enough good people in this world that will seek to do the "right thing." They may not be "good" as in Christian good because there is none that is good except God. Just good in knowing what is right versus what is wrong and that people will have a nature to want to do what is good for the nation. The statement of the belief that enough good people will do what is right was born out of the fact that eighty-plus million people voted to elect a new President and 306 electoral voters were won. Thus making "But I don't want to be the President" a reality.

It is difficult to believe that President Trump cannot accept the fact that he lost the election. How can anyone come to a realization that he won when he alienated so many people. He alienated friends, appointees, Senators, family members, the men and women of our armed forces, prisoners of war (Senator John McCain), he alienated the migrants (separating and jailing children and adults), and he alienated people of color, especially Black Americans. All of these alienations and he expected and is disappointed because the people and the states of these people did not support him?

Four years will not be enough time to allow people to forget what President Donald Trump did to this nation. The Republican Party would do itself a favor by not selecting him to represent the party as a candidate for the office of President in 2024. I can only hope that they will listen and come to the realization that the Republican Party is better off without a Donald Trump.

I am of the old school of music and as a teenager I would listen to a song written by Percy Sledge. The title was: "If Loving You Is Wrong, I Don't Wanna Be Right." Donald Trump's campaign theme was: "Make America Great Again."

One does not make America great by dividing the citizens. One does not make America great by abandoning the states that make up

America during a pandemic. One does not make America great by not showing sympathy during illnesses and sicknesses of mass citizens. One does not make America great by withdrawing from its allies. One does not make America great by ignoring its laws and documents such as the Constitution. One does not make America great by staging a coup and encouraging rioters to break the law. If these things are the attempt to Make America Great Again (MAGA) then I don't want America to be great.

At this point of the writing it is important to ask: What legacy will this President leave for others to see/read about? Will it only be a legacy of how he enhanced other rich people of his class? Will it be a legacy of how he divided the families of migrants and caged up the children and adults? Will it be his attempt to build walls of division between immigrants, races, the national government, the world's allies, and the country of Mexico? Will it be for lowering the respect the United States has enjoyed for 245 years and written in our important documents that have been in place to direct our country since this country existed as a nation? Or perhaps he will be remembered for his relationship with Putin. Above all he will be remembered for the death of the many citizens who died from the coronavirus pandemic, or worse yet, he will be remembered for the coup that he incited against the American Government and the new name that he established for himself; THE NEW BIN LADEN, the leader of the in-country terrorist group.

It is critical to notice that none of the proposed legacies are in the area of positiveness, so I have asked myself: What has Donald Trump done for the country or for the overall American people? One always wants to find something good/positive to say about a person. I could not arrive at any. Thus I will make a visceral attempt to come up with something that may give a positive twist on his achievements as President. Here it is: Maybe President Trump can create a Trump Dictionary that will contain the following words:

Anger	*Norm Buster*
Conspiracy	*Non-Conceding*
Corrupt	*Pouting*
Denial	*Proud Boys*
Doubter	*QAnon*
Drain the Swamp	*Sow Disbelief*
Fake News	*Stand Back*
Fraud	*Stand By*
Golf Spree	*Stolen Election*
Hoax	*Suffering People (Death/Virus)*
Liar	*Sulking*
Lock Her/Him Up	*Tweeter*
Coup	*Insurrection*
Loser (50 to 60 Times)	*You're on Your Own (States)*
Make America Great Again	*White Supremacy (KKK)*
Terrorist	*American Traitor*

The above proposed Trump Dictionary cannot be exhaustive and will always remain incomplete as long as Donald Trump is around.

Maybe President Donald Trump can review his failures, such as in: Coronavirus Pandemic, Declaring Election a Fraud, Lawsuits Failures, Establishing Friendships, Getting Reelected, Court Cases Overturned, Obtaining Criminal Offenses Against Joe Biden's son, Quid Quo Quan, Wall Building (Mexico), Marriages, Criminal Cases he is facing after leaving office, and the 597,785 deaths from the coronavirus. These will keep him busy enough in the years to come and may not provide time for him to run for President in 2024.

In drawing this writing to a conclusion I want to direct our attention to a statement made by the President regarding his late deceased brother. He said: "I loved my brother, and I will see him again." I am so happy that he loves someone other than himself.

I pray that his brother is in heaven where there will be a rejoicing in heaven over one sinner that repents. He will see him again, the question is where? I pray that Donald Trump's brother was a Christian, one who believed in Jesus as his personal Lord and Savior. I did not know President Trump's brother, thus I cannot judge him in his life or in his faith and thus do not know where his brother is spending eternity. We are instructed by Scripture not to judge. However, I do know Donald Trump and I know him by his words and his actions. Through his words he has stated on several occasions that "he has nothing to ask forgiveness for." I know by his action that he has no respect for the church in that he does not know the correct way to hold the Bible. I know him by the way he treats others. I know him by his lack of respect for decency and the wellbeing of others. He is a man who needs to ask forgiveness.

The Scripture tells us that: "All have sinned and fallen short of the glory of God" (Romans 3:23). First John 1:10 says, "If we say we have not sinned, we make Him a liar and the Word is not in us." From this I would submit to the readers that it is true that Donald Trump will see his brother again. The question is where will that vision of sight be held?

Hear the Parable of the Rich Man and Lazarus from Luke 16:19–31. I strongly encourage the President to read this section of Scripture with the Holy Bible right side up. I will paraphrase the Parable: There was a certain rich man who was clothed in purple and fine linen and he dined well every day. No name is given to this rich man so he could be you or he could be me; he could be Donald Trump. There was another man in this parable, and he was a beggar and his name was Lazarus. He begged the crumbs that fell from the rich man's table; however, the dogs came and licked the poor beggar's sores. The dogs showed more care and concern for the poor beggar Lazarus than the rich man did.

As will occur to each of us, so it occurred to Lazarus and the rich man. They both succumb to death. Lazarus died and was carried by the angels into the bosom of Abraham. Lazarus went to heaven, not because he was poor and a beggar but because he believed in Jesus as his personal Lord and Savior. The rich man also died, and the Bible says: "He was buried and he lifted up his eyes in hell." Not because he was rich but because he did not believe in Jesus as his personal Lord and Savior. He did not love the Lord our God with all his heart, soul, mind and strength and he did not love his neighbor as himself.

It is at this point and time that the rich man wants mercy and kindness to be shown to him. So he asked for two favors. One, that Lazarus be permitted to come and dip his finger in some water for one drop to be placed on the rich man's tongue for coolness. This is not granted. So he asked the second favor. That Lazarus be allowed to go to his father's house and tell his five brothers to change their lifestyles so that they don't come to where the rich man is.

This request is also denied with the statement that they should listen to those called to bring the message of salvation. Hear those who preach and teach the Word of the Gospel that Jesus is the way, the truth, and the life and no one comes to the Father but by Jesus.

President Trump, confess your sins, seek God's forgiveness, amend your sinful life and ways, and acknowledge Jesus as your personal Lord and Savior, do the things that are right in God's sight for your soul's salvation and for all the people of America.

www.ingramcontent.com/pod-product-compliance
Lightning Source LLC
Chambersburg PA
CBHW071333210526
45161CB00006B/13